IN QUIET MOMENTS:

A 52-Week Devotional Journal

By

Alwanda Fuqua Carothers

To Sis. Ruth
In Christian Love
+ God bless you

Alwanda F. Carothers
9/10/17

IN QUIET MOMENTS:
A 52-WEEK DEVOTIONAL JOURNAL
© 2017 By Alwanda Fuqua Carothers
ISBN 978-1533667304

Cover Illustration: ©pixbox77
Stock Photo ID: 185366149 — istock.com
Cover Design: Angela D. Valentine

DEDICATION

This book is dedicated to my Heavenly Father and to His children all over the world. To my husband, William, who has loved me unconditionally throughout our many years together; to my daughters, Kiya and Leah who have given me much delight watching them become strong women and wonderful mothers; to my grandchildren, Jamel, Jade, Jayla, and William Joquel, who bring me inexpressible joy because they are compassionate, kind, polite, and loving; to my great-grand children, Jamari and Justice who bring smiles to my face each time I see them; and to the generations to come.

It is dedicated to my parents, Allen and Ruby Fuqua, and to my grandparents, Curtis and Carrie Mae Simmons, who are no longer with us. They were instrumental in showing me how to love God, my husband, my children, and my fellow man.

It is dedicated to my siblings, Harold, Richard and Altonja (Chelle) Fuqua. They have been and continue to be blessings.

It is dedicated to all the missionaries who bravely go out to places unfamiliar spreading the Word of God, and to the countries that have opened up to those missionaries. To our spiritual family in Guyana, South America who always make William and I feel at home while being away from home.

It is also dedicated to those who are struggling with their faith. Prayerfully these devotions will build you up, encourage you, and give you strength to press on no matter the struggle.

ACKNOWLEDGEMENTS

I want to first thank my Heavenly Father for His written Word and loving me more than I can ever imagine. I thank my Lord and Savior Jesus Christ for sacrificing His sinless body on behalf of my sinful body. I thank the Holy Spirit for dwelling in my temple and for bringing the Word back to my memory when I decide to walk in my own way.

I want to thank my family, friends, and every person God has seen fit to put into my life for a reason, a season, or for a lifetime. I thank God for each of you. I want to thank my spiritual family at the Lawrence Avenue church of Christ for constantly motivating my spiritual growth.

I want to thank my editor, Jessica Emerson, whose dedication to this endeavor is very much appreciated. Your input has helped make this book a better read while keeping the intent of its context. I thank Angela Valentine for her encouragement and helping me through the self-publishing process.

I want to thank Angela Carothers, Anita Fitzgerald, Benjamin Roberts, Minister of West Eastland church of Christ, Constance Coleman Singleton, Kiya Reed, Michael and Terre Farris, Richard Fuqua, and Yvette Sharp Bussell for taking time out of your busy schedule to review Weeks 1-10. I want to thank Eula Hendricks and Tracey Spencer for proofing it. I thank you all for the encouraging words and support you so lovingly give. A special thank you to Leah Carothers, who read the entire manuscript.

- Alwanda

PREFACE

I'm a woman of simple words, but with the help of God, His word, and the guidance of His Spirit, this inspiring 52-week Devotional Journal has finally been produced. Its backstory alone speaks volumes of myself. I see God as having foreordained this work over 25 years ago when I first had the inspiration. However, through the years, I often fought the idea because of insecurity and unbelief. Yes, I found much joy in writing, but I doubted that I could write such a book that could help others. A voice of doubt was in my head constantly whispering, "I don't have a wide-range vocabulary. I'm not a Bible scholar. What do I have to say? There are other talents and interests to help the Body of Christ, so just ignore this idea." However, I have felt continually nudged by God, family, and friends to accomplish this task. At long last, at this moment, I rejoice that I surrendered to God's will and calling! This book is finished! May you as the reader also be blessed to soon say, "I've completed the task before me."

The Bible is filled with examples of God not only giving individuals tasks to complete, but also providing all that they needed to accomplish them. This book is the result of God providing me with what I needed to complete this task. I am so thankful and humbled to be a vehicle for God to work through to bless your life and your walk with His Son. Now, as you read and work through these Devotionals, I pray you will be touched spiritually. May your relationship with God and others grow daily, and may your faith increase more and more.

These Devotionals were written from a heart of love (Agape) to help those who want to have a deeper and meaningful relationship with the Heavenly Father, His Son, His Spirit, and with others. Before you read the daily devotions, I ask that you be in a quiet space and go the Father in fervent prayer. Prayer is essential so that your mind will be clear of distractions, and so that you will be able to get the intended message.

To achieve the richest blessings from your study, I want to offer these suggestions of use. (1) Use those few but vital minutes after each reading to write your personal journal thoughts. On the page entitled "In Your Quiet Moments," document how the words have affected, encouraged, inspired, or even challenged you. Be honest with yourself. Honesty is one of the keys to building meaningful relationships with God and others. (2) As a cognitive exercise, use the Bible to find scriptures that fit the **biblical principle(s)** in each Devotional.

Remember, journal all your thoughts and scriptures. One day you will not only return to this book for inspiration and encouragement, but you will find an inexpressible joy waiting for you. This book, fully used, will become a great tool for tracking your growth through the years as a child of God.

God bless you all.

TABLE OF CONTENTS

Week 1   A Storm's A-coming | 1

Week 2   The Beauty that Fades and Fades Not | 5

Week 3   "That Woman" | 9

Week 4   A Powerful Weapon and Its Accomplice | 13

Week 5   Love Covers… | 15

Week 6   Working Out | 19

Week 7   Perfume or Skunk: How Do I Smell? | 21

Week 8   A Woman's Journey | 25

Week 9   Virtue | 29

Week 10   My Favorite Season (Time Brings Change) | 31

Week 11   A Parable of the Neglectful Vinedresser | 33

Week 12   To Be or Not To Be | 37

Week 13   Fireworks | 41

Week 14   Temptation Is It Necessary? | 45

Week 15   Loving Me For Me | 47

Week 16   Joy Stealers | 49

Week 17   What I Don't Know Won't Hurt Me | 51

Week 18   What Life Throws Us | 53

Week 19   A Parable of The Disconnected Co-worker | 55

Week 20   The Weeping Willow | 59

Week 21   Giving Satan Power | 61

Week 22   Living in Spiritual Poverty | 63

Week 23   You Are Now Entering the Danger Zone | 67

Week 24   Don't Be Afraid of the Truth | 69

Week 25   Cry Out to the Lord, and He Hears | 71

Week 26   Celebrate All Existence | 75

Week 27   A Parable of the Frustrated Driver | 77

Week 28   Handouts or Helping Hands | 81

Week 29   Whose Plan Are You Fulfilling? | 83

Week 30   Allow Me to Be Mother | 87

Week 31   Flattering Words: What Good Are They? | 91

Week 32   God Has Blinders? But He is Spirit? | 93

Week 33   Procrastination: "Friend"or "Foe" | 97

Week 34   The Vision Looking Back at You | 101

Week 35   Early Morn | 105

Week 36   True Friends: Who Has Them? | 107

Week 37   Weight of Life | 111

Week 38   Exodus From Bondage | 113

Week 39   Describing God | 117

Week 40   Out of Sight Out of Mind | 119

Week 41   Hey! Who Are You Listening To? | 123

Week 42   Wisdom Is Applied Knowledge | 125

Week 43   Lord, It's Just Too Much! | 127

Week 44   Godly Mentorship | 129

Week 45   To Yourself Be Honest | 131

Week 46   Don't Be So Quick to Judge | 135

Week 47   I Want True Love—What About You? | 139

Week 48   The Exit Signs of Life | 141

Week 49   The GPS's | 145

Week 50   Words of Wisdom You Can Use | 149

Week 51   Admirers or Tormentors | 153

Week 52   Who's There for Them? | 157

A Prayer of Gratitude | 161

A Storm's A-coming

A weather report of a bad snowstorm is heading our way. A wave of *anxiety* comes across because of the events that are about to happen—grocery stores running over with shoppers—food becoming scarce on the shelves. The traffic is already horrendous—drivers trying to get to the grocery stores and to home before the bad weather hits. Lines at the gas stations are ridiculously long—got to fill up before hitting the traffic. Some stations have already run out of gas. Schools dismissed early and the bus riders will arrive home way past their normal hour. Car riders are waiting to be picked up—they just may have to camp out at the school for a while or maybe overnight. Those who are home begin to *worry* about the safety of their family and friends. Then it happens! The storm hits with a fierceness. Traffic stops—no movement at all. People are trapped at the grocery stores—got food but can't get to their cars. The need to know the wellbeing of family and friends has now become very important to those waiting at home. Checking cell phones— no signal. Turning on the TVs and radios—nothing but static. Listening closely for just a whisper of someone's voice!

Then the thought hits the mind. All the most valuable blessings we take for granted (family and friends) along with the technological luxuries we put so much trust in are simply not available. No cell phones, no TVs, no radios, and no cars. We have access to them all, but they have no value now. A trust that is tried and true is *trust in God*. Not in man or the things created by man. When nothing is available and no one is there—*God is*.

Sometimes we have to experience frightening and unsure times such as this to direct us back to Him and remember the importance of family and friends. So, love and trust God. *Love* and *appreciate* family and friends even those we don't talk to very often because God gave them to us. The family institution is so important that *He even puts the lonely in them*.

Thought for this week: Look at everything and everyone with awe, appreciation, and thankfulness. All are blessings from God.

IN YOUR QUIET MOMENTS

Who and what are you appreciating this week? Why?

_____

_____

_____

_____

_____

_____

_____

_____

_____

_____

_____

_____

_____

_____

_____

_____

_____

_____

The Beauty that Fades and Fades Not

A young lady once thought she was ugly and had nothing going for her—no redeeming qualities. She had no outward beauty. She had not accomplished many noteworthy things. She was never complimented nor encouraged by family or friends for the things she did accomplish. Because she was not outwardly beautiful, they felt there was nothing else going for her. This caused her to have very low self-esteem. However, she did have great things going for her—she was very bright, made awesome grades in school, and had a personality that captivated many. Yet sadly, she desired to be beautiful more than she desired to be smart and captivating. She graduated high school without having one date; she even went to her prom alone—that took much courage. Because she was so bright, she received a full scholarship at a prestigious college.

The first day she arrived, she met a guy who was blind and had been since birth. Although he could not see, his other senses were very sharp. This meeting sparked the beginning of a wonderful friendship. At first, she thought his friendship was credited to his blindness. "Surely, if he could see me, he wouldn't be my friend," she thought to herself. As time went by and their relationship deepened, they did everything together outside of school and work.

One day the young man got up the nerve to ask if she would consider dating him. He had wanted to approach her with this idea for a while, but he hesitated because he thought she would turn him down because of his handicap. She thought about his question and asked him why he wanted to turn their friendship into a dating relationship. He told her that his feelings had deepened beyond friendship for quite some time. He always thought about the first time they met; how **gentle and kind her voice** was, how he was affected by her captivating personality, her cheerful **spirit**, and much to her surprise, even her overall **beauty**. His earnest words touched her soul deeply. Someone actually thought she was not only kind and gentle, but also beautiful. Needless to say, she had feelings for him as well and they started dating with a hopeful, bright, and loving future ahead.

Thought for this week: Remember that outside beauty fades, but inner beauty remains and shines brighter when cultivated with the Word of God. Keep cultivating your **inward beauty** because it will be **seen by the Unseen** (God).

IN YOUR QUIET MOMENTS

How will you cultivate your inward beauty this week?
What is the Unseen seeing in you?

_____

_____

_____

_____

_____

_____

_____

_____

_____

_____

_____

_____

_____

_____

_____

_____

_____

"That Woman"

There have been so many times in my life when storms have come. Storms so devastating I didn't know how I was going to make it through them (physically, mentally, and spiritually). Just like the tornados or hurricanes in nature, there is always the **EYE** of the storm—where quietness and calmness reside. But getting through the storm to get to the Eye is sometimes difficult, especially when you are trying to weather it alone. Just when it seems like you won't be able to make it to the Eye, while the storm is fierce and raging, God sends "That Woman." How did she know to call just to say, "hello?"

"That Woman" who loves God brings her friend with her whether during phone conversations or making physical visits. They both listen as I talk through my anger and fear. She comforts me as I push through my many tears. She and her friend are both there during the storm, and they stay to help me until I reach the Eye. "That Woman" is also there in spirit when not in person; she is constantly praying for me, and believe me I feel the effects of her prayers. What a blessing it is to finally reach the Eye where there is quiet and calm! However, another storm begins to brew on the other side of the Eye. And you know what? God sends "That Woman" again!

We all need that someone in our lives that can ***pray for us*** and surround us with godly fellowship. I have "That Woman" in my life. Her friend is always with her. I am so thankful to God that I have "That Woman" in my life, and that she always has her friend with her. I know her eyes are reading this as well. I pray that just as she's "That Woman" for me, I can be "That Woman" for others and bring my friend also. Oh by the way, that *friend* is *JESUS*!

Thought for this week: Be thankful for "That Person" in your life. Be "That Person" for others, and never forget to take your friend JESUS along with you. They will need you both.

Who is "That Person" in your life and what does he or she mean to you? You may have many, and that's a blessing! How are you preparing to be "That Person" for someone this week? Are you taking your friend with you?

_____

_____

_____

_____

_____

_____

_____

_____

_____

_____

_____

_____

_____

_____

_____

A Powerful Weapon and Its Accomplice

Do you know you possess a powerful weapon? It is with you every day and with every step. It is so powerful that, if used incorrectly, it can slash like a knife, slap one senseless, and leave you speechless. It can cause one to bend towards the ground in despair and shame, or destroy masses of people at one time. It can be used as a ploy for deception, for taking advantage, and for manipulation. But when used correctly, it can build, repair, and restore. It can bring contentment to the desperate. It can bring comfort to the dying soul. It can direct a lost, mournful soul to a safe haven. It can sooth the hurt, and calm the angry masses.

What is this weapon that we possess which can do so much damage, yet do so much good? The weapon is the **TONGUE!** However, it does not perform alone. It has an accomplice—the **OPENED MOUTH**! So, when we open our mouths, let's make sure what comes out of it will **benefit the listeners** and not be used to lie, harm, kill, or destroy.

Thought for this week: The tongue is powerful. Focus on the heart to use the tongue carefully and correctly. If not, it might just backfire.

How will you use your powerful weapon this week? Are you taking the time to think before you open your mouth? What words are you using to uplift and encourage someone?

_____

_____

_____

_____

_____

_____

_____

_____

_____

_____

_____

_____

_____

_____

_____

_____

LOVE COVERS...

...when someone betrays a confidence.

...when someone cuts you off in traffic or blows their horn before you can pull through the light.

...when your friend decides not to speak to you anymore, treats you like the plague, and you don't know why.

...when your children hurt you by not keeping in touch.

...when a church member speaks ill of you and causes other church members to have the same ideas.

...when your children ignore their spiritual upbringing.

...when your spouse admits he or she is having an affair or battling with pornography or other addictions.

...when your boss shows favoritism or overlooks you for a promotion or pay increase.

I have to pause here to ask: *AM I TALKING TO ANYONE YET?*

...when someone sees you waiting for a parking spot and zips in ahead of you.

...when a clerk sees you having trouble locating a certain store item, but just stands there looking at you or rudely rolling his or her eyes if you ask for help.

...when someone tries to crush or destroy your spirit.

...when you are in line first and the server overlooks you and serves someone else instead.

...when you have an abusive spouse (mentally or physically).

...when your best friend moves away and you become the one doing all the calling.

...when you are always giving, and others are always taking.

...when you love someone with all your being, and it is not reciprocated.

LOVE (AGAPE—unconditional love) COVERS A MULTITUDE OF SIN.

Thought for this week: It's sad to say, but it's true: not everybody loves (Agape). Do something wrong, and you will see wrath versus love. Show the love of God no matter what happens this week, as much as it lies within you to do so.

IN YOUR QUIET MOMENTS

List some things that tested love (Agape) this week.
How are you exemplifying love in the face adversity?
How are others showing love towards you?

_____

_____

_____

_____

_____

_____

_____

_____

_____

_____

_____

_____

_____

_____

_____

_____

_____

_____

Working Out

There are those who spend hours and hours every day working out and doing things to help keep their body fit and healthy. Fitness is just as important to them as food and water. They do this to sustain their physical health and prolong the quality of their lives. But, I have news for you—the act of ***BODILY EXERCISE PROFITS LITTLE!***

What!? You mean to tell me that I'm spending all of this time and energy, and experiencing all of this pain, sweat, and soreness, but that it's doing me little good.

Yes, bodily exercise is good, but it profits little! However, let me encourage you. There is a workout that profits much! We should be doing this as often as we can: the ***working out of your own soul's salvation.*** Working out in godliness (learning how to live a godly life) is valuable in EVERY way to the body and the soul. When your soul is healthy, your body will also be healthy. This workout holds a promise for this present life and the time beyond.

Thought for this week: Bodily exercise promises benefits in the present life, but cannot promise anything in the afterlife.

Evaluate your workout this week. How much time is spent on bodily exercise that profits little, compared to the time spent working out in godliness that benefits beyond the present throughout eternity?

_____

_____

_____

_____

_____

_____

_____

_____

_____

_____

_____

_____

_____

_____

_____

Perfume or Skunk:
How Do I Smell?

Perfume smells wonderful! You can get a variety of pleasing fragrances: floral (scent of flowers), oriental (scent of spice), chypre (earthy, woodsy scent), green (scent of fresh green grass), oceanic (scents of sandy beach, clean), and many others. We have all experienced these scents at one time or another; they have a nice, appealing, and soothing effect on us. However, when a skunk is agitated, it emits an odor that smells horrible. Hopefully, one doesn't die under your house or get hit by your car! The smell lingers for days and can be smelled a mile away! The smell can actually make some people ill. I have asked myself, why can't the nice smell of perfume last as long as a stinky skunk's smell does?

As I think about these two scents, I can't help but think about myself. Physically speaking, I intentionally put on perfume because I want to have a pleasant aroma around people. I want to attract people, not repel them. But spiritually speaking, how do I want to smell to God and my fellow man?

Do I bring a sweet aroma (friendly, loving, approachable) with me that attracts, or do I bring a stench (rudeness, hatefulness, unapproachable) that repels? I have to ask myself, do people want to be around me or do they stay away? How is my spirit going to smell? You and I have a choice each day. I've decided I'm going to intentionally bring the *sweet aroma* (love, joy, peace, forbearance, kindness, goodness, faithfulness, gentleness, and self-control) before God, to be found pleasing before Him and my fellow man. When my spirit smells godly and sweet, everyone—even God—will have a pleasing experience being around me.

Thought for this week: Having a sweet aroma in the spirit will attract people, and having a hateful one will repel them.

What aroma will you bring with you this week? If it is a sweet one, what kind of effect does it have on those around you? If it is a stinky one, what kind of effect does it have on those around you?

_____

_____

_____

_____

_____

_____

_____

_____

_____

_____

_____

_____

_____

_____

_____

_____

_____

A Woman's Journey

The woman's journey over time has seen its challenges and changes. She was a mother and a wife (a full-time job) who took care of the home and family; she transitioned from home to replace the drafted men in the workplace; after some time of proving capable of doing a man's job, perhaps even better than some men, she decided to continue outside employment and allow others to tend to the responsibilities of her home and family. As time progressed, she became highly educated and ran huge corporations, which added more responsibilities and tremendous stress to her plate.

Although she had apparently "made it" to the top of the ladder of success, did she choose to slow down for family life? Sadly not, since the temptation was too strong to maintain her lifestyle. She had even become so accustomed to the busy rat race, and the hustle and challenges of her career, that she would miss it so much and her home life would seem uneventful or unfulfilling. Yet, since the strengthening of her family was at risk due to her absence and work life, the guilt she now feels brings on more stress. Something went wrong somewhere—but where?

Much to our detriment, society has made it easier for roles to be both switched and confused—JUST LOOK AROUND! Take note—women are dying at an increased rate of heart disease. Today it is considered the #1 killer of women. You were not built to take on such stress. Woman, do you know or remember why you were created? Let me share to answer with you—**you were created for man as his helper, to bear children**, and **to be keepers of the home**. Some of us have stepped out of our God-purposed role. You must allow the man to do what he was created to do—to **work by the sweat of his brow** and shoulder those stresses of life. Lord, please forgive us for we know not what we do.

Thought for this week: If you are married, leave the leadership, stresses, and hard work to your husband, and prayerfully, he will receive his guidance from God. If you are single, most likely you have to work, but for leadership lean on God, for stresses give them to Christ, and for guidance listen to the Holy Spirit.

Who will you allow to lead you this week—Husband, God, Christ, Holy Spirit? When you do, what happens? When you don't, what happens?

_____

_____

_____

_____

_____

_____

_____

_____

_____

_____

_____

_____

_____

_____

_____

_____

_____

Virtue

I love the word *virtue!* It means being the best YOU that you can be and doing the best you can do in ALL aspects of life. I try to express the importance of this characteristic to all young people who I come in contact with by words as well as example. It's never too early to teach or practice virtue because it teaches moral goodness, integrity, respect, decency, dignity, principles, ethics, and excellence. As virtue is being developed throughout life, the essential desire will be to become the best child, student, sibling, friend, employee, spouse, etc. YOU can be. Most importantly, you will want to be the best Christian you can be! By no means does this mean being perfect—there was only one perfect man that walked the face of the earth, and that was Jesus Christ. But it does mean being the best YOU that you can be. Take a look at a *virtuous woman*; such godly conduct makes one a great example of being the best HER that she could be.

Thought for the week: VIRTUE is something we all should possess because the world needs more of it.

Did you show the traits or characteristics of virtue this week? If so, what are some of the things you are doing to incorporate virtue in your life?

_____

_____

_____

_____

_____

_____

_____

_____

_____

_____

_____

_____

_____

_____

_____

_____

WEEK 10
My Favorite Season
(Time Brings Change)

Oh, the season of fall—it surely is my favorite season. So many wonderful things happen in the fall that make you pause and notice the **glorious wonder of God's creative power**. The trees change from green to yellow to orange, and many other radiant colors. The hot summer fades and the coolness of fall quickly takes its place. The air is now clean, fresh, crisp, and easier to breath. The temperature is not too hot, not too cold...juuuuust right. You can begin to the see the pace of summer's hustle diminish—things thankfully start to slow down. Pumpkins, hay bales, corn stalks, and scarecrows are now decorating the lawns and porches. The anticipation and excitement of what is ahead—upcoming holidays—the gatherings of families and friends. Oh, the season of fall!

My heart leaps for joy just thinking of the calming pleasures I get from my quiet moments observing all of this. While fall makes us stop and take notice of God's glorious wonder, it also reminds us that nothing stays the same—nature changes and so do I. As I get older, I'm constantly changing in body, mind, and spirit. So, as fall brings change to the trees with bright colors and the coolness brings freshness to every breath, I pray that my life brings that type of radiant and refreshing blessing to a wandering, struggling soul.

Thought for the week: Every season is a gift from God, and each brings an awesomeness that no man can duplicate.

IN YOUR QUIET MOMENTS

Think about your favorite season or time of the year this week. Why is it your favorite? What memories do you have about it?

_____

_____

_____

_____

_____

_____

_____

_____

_____

_____

_____

_____

_____

_____

_____

_____

_____

Parable of the Neglectful Vinedresser

There was a Vinedresser who had the richest vineyard in all of the land. That land was so fertile that it grew the most plump and beautiful grapes anybody had ever seen. People from all over the area came to see the vineyard and to purchase his grapes at harvest time. He loved this vineyard, and it was something he was proud of because he put all his time and effort into it to make it what it was. He also prayed for the right type of weather and ***God always answered*** his prayers at just the right time.

Eventually, some things happened that took the vinedresser's attention from the vineyard. He got married, had children, acquired other businesses, and other people demanded his time. Because the vineyard was so rich and produced an overabundance of grapes every year, he didn't think it needed much care. So, because there were other things that were more important, the vinedresser only had time to do the minimum work required. He believed it would still produce as usual.

Now as time went by, the vinedresser only did what was necessary to get by. He didn't put the love, time or care into the vineyard as he once did. He even forgot to pray for the right weather. One day, he went out to the vineyard and discovered the vineyard was dried up...there were no more plump, beautiful grapes to harvest. The vineyard was no more. This made the vinedresser very despondent and distraught because he realized what he had done and did not do.

Thought for the week: There are several messages within this parable, but I'm talking about the destruction of relationships. Without prayer and nurturing, relationships can also dry up and die. Don't be like the neglectful vinedresser and expect your relationships to keep growing and producing without love, time, care, nurture, and most of all PRAYER. Keep in mind, that just like the vineyard, relationships dry up and die too.

Evaluate ALL your relationships this week. Do you notice that some of them are not as strong as they used to be? Are you nurturing them or neglecting them? If you don't know, ask.

To Be or Not To Be?

To be happy or not be
To be sad or not be
To be loving or not be
To be hateful or not be
To be forgiving or not be
To be resentful or not be
To be married or not be
To be divorced or not be
To be a virgin or not be
To be a fornicator or not be
To be a glutton or not be
To be thankful or not be
To be selfish or not be
To be humble or not be
*To be **prideful** or not be*
To be truthful or not be
To be a liar or not be
To be giving or not be
To be a taker or not be
*To be a **submissive wife**/loving husband be or not be*
To be a mistress or not be
To be a good worker or not be
To be a slacker or not be
To be a procrastinator or not be
To be kind or not be
To be lazy or not be
To be wise or not be
To be ignorant or not be
To be a seeker of truth or not be
To be a believer in God or not be
To be a sinner or not be
To be repentant or not be
To be a Christian or not be

Thought for the week: We are constantly faced with to be or not be. If you choose to do that which is against God's character and will, don't beat yourself up pray, repent, and move on.

Write down some things you are struggling with this week. Are you struggling with the "to be or not to be" question? Don't feel like you are alone, because we all struggle with this question. Do you know why you are struggling? How are you dealing with your struggle(s) so you can move on?

_____

_____

_____

_____

_____

_____

_____

_____

_____

_____

_____

_____

_____

_____

Fireworks

In my quiet moment, I remember the firework displays I have seen over the years. They were so many and so beautiful! The sight of them can take your breath away. The sky was lit so bright with colored fire. How do they pull off such a spectacular event? I saw a documentary once on how these displays are orchestrated and the many people involved to make sure of its safety and success. There is an engineering team, a creative team, a combustion team, a firefighting team, and a design team. The design team knows how to combine the powders and set up the displays to go off in just the right time and right sequence. As I think about this, I think about how life can be like firework displays as well. These fireworks are not pretty, but *can* take your breath away.

As I think about the orchestration for a fireworks display, I think about the orchestration of life's fireworks. There's the creative team (those who sit back creating the situations); the engineers (those who knows what to say and do to succeed); the combustion team (those who are close by making sure the fuse does not ignite or get out of control); the design team (those who set up the occasion, making things conducive for the situation to be ignited); and there are **the firefighters** (those who come with the Word of God to extinguish the fires)—thank God for them.

Thought for the week: Satan is the one who orchestrates of all life's fireworks, so keep the combustion team and firefighters close to you so that when those fireworks come in your life, they will give you what you need, THE WORD OF GOD.

When you see fireworks brewing this week, what will you do? Are you the engineer, the creative team, the design team? Or are you the combustion team or a firefighter? What is it about the situation that encourages you to join one or more of the teams?

_____

_____

_____

_____

_____

_____

_____

_____

_____

_____

_____

_____

_____

_____

_____

_____

Temptation Is It Necessary?

Does it seem like you are tempted more than you would like to be? Why do we have to be tempted at all? *Why won't Satan just leave us alone*? Oh no, he's not going to do that! He has something to accomplish before his time runs out...and he realizes that his time is limited. In my quiet moment, I understand why temptations exist. However, understanding why does not always make one feel confident in their walk with God--sometimes we fall into temptation, and sometimes we fall really hard.

Temptations are necessary because our responses to them will show us where we are spiritually. Being faced with those temptations and having the ability to overcome them will keep us humble and more submissive to God and His Word. If they overtake us, we must quickly have a heart of repentance before we get so far that it will be difficult to see the wrong we are doing. I must say here, that if we are the tempter, STOP IT! Our soul will be in more danger if we are the tempter than it would be if we are the tempted. *Even though we are tempted, be encouraged; God always gives us a way of escape*. However, we must be aware of the escapes He provides and be strong enough to adhere to them.

Thought for this week: It is not beneficial to you or anyone else if you fall into temptation. In fact, it can be detrimental. If you do fall, don't stay there; if you do, you will get stuck, and it will be harder to break free.

Are you recognizing the escapes that God is providing
this week when you are tempted? What are the
temptations, and what are the escapes that God
provides?

_____

_____

_____

_____

_____

_____

_____

_____

_____

_____

_____

_____

_____

_____

_____

_____

WEEK 15
Loving Me For Me

In one of my quiet moments, I asked myself, do I really love ME? Society says you're too dark or too light, you're too tall or too short, you're too fat or too thin, you're the wrong race, you're not educated enough, you're in the wrong family, you're too poor or too rich, too pretty or too ugly—it goes on and on and on. According to society, having these flaws means you are unlovable and that you don't fit. And we know that whatever society thinks and says is GOSPEL.

If you are one who listens to society and has a hard time loving yourself, I'm here to tell you that it's time to stop lending your ear to society and start listening to God. You are His creation. ***He formed you in the womb and formed you perfectly to His specifications***, so start the process of loving yourself today. It is NOT easy, and it won't happen overnight. It all begins with loving God first, and understanding and trusting His love for you. His love is unconditional, trustworthy and sure. ***He doesn't see the outward appearance of man, He sees the inward man***. As you understand and trust this magnificent love, you can then turn that love towards yourself. When you love yourself unconditionally, you can begin loving others unconditionally as well.

Thought for this week: Understanding the love of your Maker is the beginning of loving yourself. This love is important and pleasing to your Maker because when you love yourself, you will love others as God has loved you.

How are you showing love this week, i.e. patience, kindness, protection, etc.? How are you being shown love? Have you been unloving this week, i.e. easily angered, delighting in evil, envying, etc.?

_____

_____

_____

_____

_____

_____

_____

_____

_____

_____

_____

_____

_____

_____

_____

_____

Week 16
Joy Stealers

Feeling disappointed and discouraged? These are joy-stealers that Satan uses against the children of God. Disappoint us, discourage us, and you find a wounded and withered soul. What can you do, and how can you heal and find joy again? *Pray and get strength from God's Word, and have a forgiving heart.* Never expect joy to come to you from your environment; joy comes from within. I remember a song I used to sing when I was a child: "I've got joy, joy, joy, joy, down in my heart, down in my heart, down in my heart. I've got joy, joy, joy, joy, down in my heart. Down in my heart to stay." Joy in the heart is a joy that surpasses all understanding. *Tears may occupy the night, but joy comes with the morning.* I choose to have joy. What about you?

Thought for the week: Find joy in the Lord, and you will not have to depend on the counterfeit joy offered by the world.

Will you find joy that surpasses all understanding this week? Where are you looking for this joy? Do you recognize the difference between real and counterfeit joy?

Week 17
What I Don't Know Won't Hurt Me

Why do people not read the Word of God? There can be several reasons. One can be they don't read it for fear of seeing themselves. If they see that they are not in line with the Word, they will feel the conviction to make changes. Another can be that they have the misguided thought "what I don't know won't hurt me." But what people don't realize is that not knowing *will* hurt you. It will hurt your soul! God has said that there is no longer an excuse not to live a life acceptable to Him because ***He has given us everything we need pertaining to life and godliness.*** There was a time He winked at our ignorance, but He will not any longer. Dear Friends, how do we know we are not pleasing to God if we are not told? So, read the Word of God, for within it is LIFE that leads to salvation.

Thought for the week: Read the Word of God to find out what He expects from His creation. Read it and live.

Did you read the Word of God (the Bible) this week? What are you learning? Are you learning new things and reinforcing old knowledge? Are you incorporating those things into your life?

_____

_____

_____

_____

_____

_____

_____

_____

_____

_____

_____

_____

_____

_____

_____

Week 18
What Life Throws Us

Life can throw us both light and heavy loads to bear. We consciously give the light loads to God to carry. We can go about our day not thinking or being concerned about them—all things are well—God has this. However, when it comes to heavier ones, we don't handle them quite the same way. They are weightier and affect us big time, and we probably feel as though we are bearing them alone. No, it's not easy to go about our day not thinking or being overly concerned about them. Sometimes we allow them to stagnate us and we can't let go. But do you realize we are saying that God can handle only the light matters and not the heavier ones?

If you are aware that you are giving God only the light loads to carry for you, be courageous and give Him the heavy ones too. You may ask, "How?" Let me encourage you to take one day at a time and consciously and purposefully *give all things to the One who can carry and handle the light and heavy loads of life*. When you do this and totally let go, you will experience an unexplainable peace and witness things being worked out without your input or help. Give to and leave them with God. Praise and thank Him for His peace.

Thought for the week: Giving our cares to God is the best decision we can make. He will take care of them all. Trust Him to do that.

IN YOUR QUIET MOMENTS

Has life thrown you unexpected challenges this week? What are they, and how did you handle them? Are you handling them yourself? Which ones are you handling, and which have you given to God?

A Parable of The Disconnected Co-worker

There was a young woman who moved from her home state for a better paying job. She went to work every day for months, and even though she loved what she did and was around a lot of people in her office, she felt alone and disconnected. There were many differences—race, lifestyle, religious belief—and she wondered if this was the reason for the disconnection. However, these differences did not personally affect her, her work ethics, or her ability to reach out. The atmosphere was loud and disrespectful. There were offensive words used so much that you would think it was a job requirement for that particular area. There were no holds barred when it came to the types of conversations these people had: they shared things about their personal lives, spouses, children, financial difficulties, etc. The young woman did not feel like a part of most of the conversations because she could not add to them, nor did she feel that she could make a difference.

Frequently, she was told how valuable she was to the team and to the company. You would think, since she was so valuable, she would feel more connected—not disconnected. Every day, she left that job feeling so empty. She lived alone, and had not been in the state long enough to have friends; when she got home, the feeling of emptiness was sometimes unbearable.

One day, she looked around her apartment and listened. All she heard was silence, and she wanted it to stop. She turned on the TV and the radio—still silence. She no longer wanted to hear the silence or to feel disconnected and lonely. She walked into her silence. She no longer wanted to hear the silence or to feel disconnected and lonely. She walked into her bedroom, changed her clothes, went into her bathroom, and looked into the mirror. She took a razor and purposefully slit her wrists. You see, the feelings of loneliness and disconnection got the best of her that day. She watched herself in the mirror, tears streaming down her face, until she slumped to the floor.

The next day, she was late coming into work. This was so unlike her and she did not call in. Everyone wondered where she was. They called her on her phone and received no answer. The next day, the same thing happened. Her supervisor became very concerned and decided to stop by her apartment. A feeling of joy came over her when saw her car in the driveway. She knocked on her door—no answer. She went to a neighbor and asked if anyone had seen her. They responded "no." The feeling of joy turned into worry, and she called the authorities. The young woman was found dead.

Thought for the week: Have you ever been the new employee, neighbor, family member, church member, or student? We've all been the new kid on the block at some point in our lives, and loneliness and disconnection could be our story too. It's not a new one—it's just a reminder. Let me encourage you to be the one person who reaches out to the new person. Be the one who changes the story from death to life.

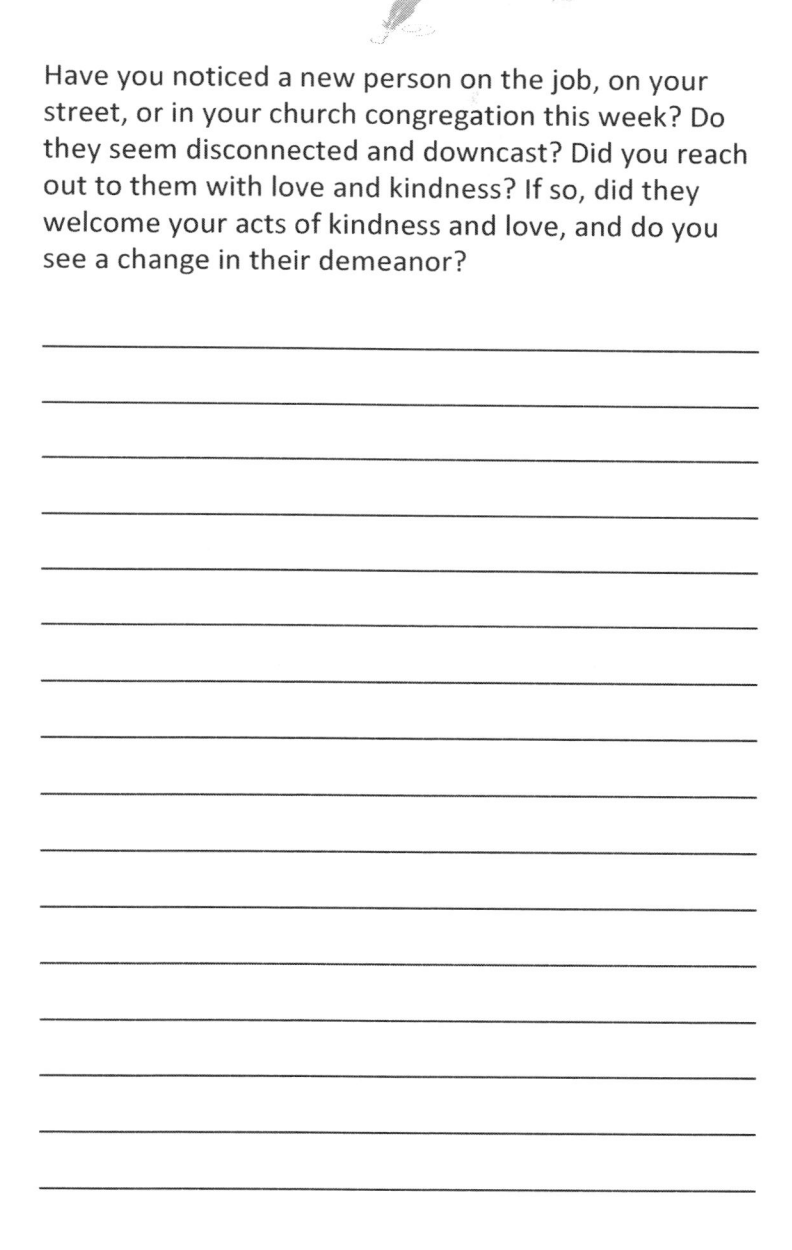

Have you noticed a new person on the job, on your street, or in your church congregation this week? Do they seem disconnected and downcast? Did you reach out to them with love and kindness? If so, did they welcome your acts of kindness and love, and do you see a change in their demeanor?

Week 20
The Weeping Willow

As I take notice of a weeping willow tree, I see how its branches droop over and how very fragile they look. They sway back and forth with the wind so elegantly, reminding me of a well-choreographed dance. Each branch knows each sway so perfectly that even the wheat is impressed and wants to join in. Who is the choreographer of such a beautiful dance? *It is God who created the weeping willow and without effort of its own, it follows His lead and the wind being the music*. We are His creation, but sometimes we get out of step.

We lose our focus because of the many distractions that keep us from hearing His directions. However, when we get back in focus, we can hear the music. It's at that moment we realize God has always been *choreographing our dance, one step at a time*, and the music is the Holy Bible.

Thought for the week: God is our creator, and He directs our steps. Don't move ahead of God, but walk alongside of Him. Sometimes He takes us places we are unsure of, but trust Him and go anyway.

IN YOUR QUIET MOMENTS

Have you allowed God to direct your steps this week? If so, where did He take you? Did you trust Him?

_____

_____

_____

_____

_____

_____

_____

_____

_____

_____

_____

_____

_____

_____

_____

_____

Week 21
Giving Satan Power

Did you know that we have a sinful nature? Did you know that we give Satan power to use that sinful nature as a weapon against us? *He roams to and fro throughout the earth like a roaring lion seeking those he can devour (destroy).* He is looking for those habits and thoughts that keep us at odds with the Creator. When Satan sees these sinful things, we have now given him power over us. Every time we sin, he stands before the angels of God with boldness and accusing us. I can hear him saying, "See what your PRECIOUS creation has done now?" He knows that sin *separates us from God*, and that when we sin we are separated from Him at that time.

Do you want to change Satan's boldness to timidity, stop his accusations, and diminish the powerful weapons he has over you? Do you want to be connected to and in harmony with the Creator? Be humble and recognize that you are a sinner, repent of your sins, confess with the mouth that Jesus Christ is the Son of God, and be buried with Him (Christ) into the watery grave of baptism that washes away your sins. When you rise with Him, you are a new creation. Satan no longer recognizes you because you have godly habits and godly thoughts. You are new creation—A CHILD OF GOD!

Thought for the week: We are the servants of sin when we allow Satan to have dominion over our lives. We are servants of righteousness when we allow God to have dominion over our lives.

Are there any sins that hold you captive and in the clutches of Satan this week? Do you recognize them? If so, what are they, and what are you doing or not doing to change your position as a servant of sin or servant of righteousness?

_____

_____

_____

_____

_____

_____

_____

_____

_____

_____

_____

_____

_____

_____

Living in Spiritual Poverty

How do you know when you are living in **spiritual poverty**? Here are some indications. If you are NOT feeding your soul daily with the book of life and godliness (The Book—the Bible—the Word of God), you are in jeopardy of spiritual poverty. If you are feeding your soul with the pleasures of this world, then you are headed for spiritual poverty. If your soul is ingesting and digesting more of the world's pleasures than it is of The Book, then you are even closer to spiritual poverty. If you are depending on someone else to feed your soul with their own spiritual ideas and opinions, then you are leaving yourself open to being led astray and having to fend for yourself. If you are sparingly (every now and then) feeding the soul with The Book and it purges what you fed it, you are now at the door of spiritual poverty and ready to walk through. Then it happens—your soul is weak, impoverished, and vulnerable to the **devouring nature of the lion** (Satan). What a sad place to be.

But, there is good news! You don't have to stay in this impoverished condition. Before your soul starves and withers, you can make some changes, and you can start today—right now! Pray for cleansing and understanding. Then begin feeding your soul spiritual food to ingest, digest, and live on daily. **Feed on, live by, and live out The Book and enjoy spiritual richness, abundance of life, health, and wealth.**

Thought for the week: Feed your soul The Book daily for within it is the nature of God, His plan for mankind, and salvation through His Son. Your soul depends on it for spiritual food in order to grow and mature as it prepares for the spiritual blessings and ultimately the promises of God.

Are you feeding on the Word of God this week? If so, how often are you ingesting the Word? Are you digesting it or purging it? What are you learning about your Creator, His Son and His Spirit? What is His plan for you? What spiritual blessings and promises are you looking forward to in this life and the life to come?

_____

_____

_____

_____

_____

_____

_____

_____

_____

_____

_____

_____

_____

_____

_____

_____

Week 23
You Are Now Entering the Danger Zone

Why is it that so many people want to know their destiny (the future)? They want to know so badly that they consult horoscopes, palm readers, dream interpreters, *mediums*, and other sources. They do not know that they are entering a Danger Zone. Don't you know that God hates these types of activities? He hated them when it was first introduced to his people centuries ago, He hates them now, and He will always hate them. They are activities of Satan. He uses them as another ploy to lead you further and further away from God. Leave your destiny to the One who created you. *He has your life all mapped out*. The life that will lead you back to Him, so trust His plan for you. Want to know your destiny? Consult God through prayer and His Word!

Thought for this week: You are entering the Danger Zone when you seek out knowledge of your destiny from sources other than God.

Have you entered the Danger Zone this week? Are you seeking your destiny from sources other than God? If so, what did you consult about? Did you consult God? How do you feel from the knowledge you obtained?

_____

_____

_____

_____

_____

_____

_____

_____

_____

_____

_____

_____

_____

_____

_____

Week 24
Don't Be Afraid of the Truth

Some people are afraid to read the Word of God because of what it may reveal. It may point out all the wrong that they have done or are now doing. Yes, God reveals the wrong to us because if He didn't, **we would not know if we were in sin**. But, dear one, there is more revealed in His Word than pointing out wrongdoings. God reveals himself, His love, His Son, His Spirit, eternal life, and gives a glimpse of Heaven—the promise land, the land flowing with milk and honey; the Word of God is the guide to show us these things and bring us to the promise land. It shows us how to love, and what it looks like to be loved. It reveals, warns, and shows us the schemes of the adversary (Satan). ***The Word is truth and knowing the truth sets us FREE!***

Thought of the week: Being told the truth is so freeing and refreshing because there are so many lies being told in the world. No one wants to be lied to or deceived.

What lies are being told to you, and what lies are you telling this week? Name them and remember that the little colored lies count too—if there is such a thing. How do you feel when someone lies to or deceives you?

_____

_____

_____

_____

_____

_____

_____

_____

_____

_____

_____

_____

_____

_____

Cry Out to the Lord, and He Hears

Have you ever cried, I mean really cried out to the Lord for help, and **_He reached down and helped you?_** I have, and believe me—my faith increases more every time.

In a quiet moment, a feeling of anxiety came over me as I remembered the time I cried out to the Lord, I mean really cried out, and He reached down and rescued me by acting through my husband. It was the year we were celebrating our 25th wedding anniversary, and a cruise to Cancun, Mexico was a gift to ourselves. We went to a beach there where we had planned to spend the day relaxing and enjoying the breeze off of the Atlantic Ocean. How beautiful it was. Hubby came up with the idea of jet skiing. I don't know how to swim, and that idea was not appealing to me; in fact, it was definitely out of the question. I rejected the invitation, but in the face of my reluctance, I decided to take the chance. It really looks like fun and others seem to be enjoying it, I said to myself; convincing myself it was going to be okay, I decided to take the chance.

All was going pretty well, when all of a sudden a big touring boat headed our way. A wave came towards us and we capsized. Oh no, Lord this can't be happening! I was moving in slow motion. There I was, in this huge body of water, and I CAN'T SWIM! I did have on a life jacket, but I didn't really know how it was suppose keep me afloat. I felt my hubby reach for me and pull me up above water—thank you Lord I was able to breathe. I looked around, and there I was helpless with thoughts of being pulled under by sharks, flooding my mind, I became overwhelmed with fear, and all I could say was *"JESUS, JESUS."* I cried out His name so many times that it seemed like a million. I tried to calm down to say a quiet prayer, but the fear overwhelmed me again and I cried aloud for His help again and again. In a time of despair and great fear, and thoughts of my hubby seeing me perish that day, ***God sent help to us***. A boat of rescue was on its way. That is a day I will never forget. I won't forget the fear or the sounds that came out of my mouth. God heard my cry that day, and He will hear you—so cry out to Him, He hears!

Thought for the week: God hears every cry of His children. Never allow Satan to convince you that He doesn't. God loves us and He will take care of us. He will rescue us in times of trouble.

Did you have to cry out to God this week? What was it about? Did He hear you? If not this week, have you ever had to cry out to Him? If so, did He hear you?

_____

_____

_____

_____

_____

_____

_____

_____

_____

_____

_____

_____

_____

_____

_____

_____

_____

_____

Week 26
Celebrate All Existence

Have you celebrated the existence of all of God's creation? You may be asking yourself, "celebrated how?" I mean treating all of His creation with love, respect, and honor because He created them. In my quiet moment, I had to ask myself the same question. Well, I thought, I celebrate the existence of the human race. I try to follow the **Golden Rule,** treating others like I want to be treated. But, after careful thought, I had to confess that there have been times, many times, that I have not done so. For some of His creations, I have a hard time celebrating and abiding by that Rule. I have to say, that because of fear I've kicked dogs and cats, despised mice and rats, and killed spiders and various other insects. I have to remember that **God gave man dominion over all the animals** to care for them, not to mistreat, kill, or despise them.

All of God's creations are precious to Him and are due love, respect, care and honor. I repent for not being a better steward. All creation has a purpose, and I pray I will remember this Rule when fear tempts me. I want to he celebrated for my existence, as all creation wants to be celebrated for theirs.

Thought for the week: Remember, God created the heavens, the earth, and everything in them. Since He created all things, all things should be celebrated because all things were created for a purpose.

Have you fulfilled your purpose this week? If so, what is your purpose and how did you carry it out? Are you celebrating the existence of all God's creation, and are you being celebrated?

_____

_____

_____

_____

_____

_____

_____

_____

_____

_____

_____

_____

_____

_____

A Parable of the Frustrated Driver

There was a man named Joe who had a sister whom he hadn't seen in a very long while. He decided to drive from Chicago, Illinois to Jacksonville, Florida to visit her. He decided to drive because he was terrified of the very thought of flying. Joe was so excited; the expectation of how it would be seeing her again was overwhelming. There would be so much joy, and oh, how the tears were going to flow. They are going to spend time together reminiscing about their childhood with family and friends—good and bad times. They were going bond again.

The day was finally here for Joe to start his eagerly awaited journey. His bags and gifts were in the car, gas tank full until the next fill up, music all ready to be played, and GPS set. As Joe was pulling out of his driveway, he could see a car in the distance, far away enough for him to have time to pull out. As Joe was pulling ahead, the person in the oncoming car began blowing his car horn from three houses away. Joe was trying to understand why this person was blowing his horn. He had enough time to pull out, but he noticed the oncoming car sped up! Joe thought, "This person needs to slow down. I hope this is not going to be the kind of adventure ahead of me." Joe pulled out of the drive, and he was now on his way.

Three blocks from the house, while sitting at a traffic light, it happened—before Joe could move his foot from the brake to the accelerator, the person in the car behind him felt the need to frantically blow his horn and rudely pulled around. "Again with the honking! I can't believe it!" Joe mouthed. A few miles later, Joe was on the interstate, driving the speed limit, and traveling in the right lane. The traffic was heavier than usual in that area for some reason; the right lane was slow and left lane was stopped. Joe looked out of his rearview mirror, and he noticed that the car behind him was right on his bumper. If Joe needed to stop suddenly, he would be hit from behind. This behavior continued until the flow of traffic was better and the other driver was able to pull around. This person laid on his horn and pulled into traffic as if he was on a speedway track. Traffic began to slow down again, and Joe was side by side with the bumper rider. Joe caught their eye, rolled his window down, and asked the driver why he felt the need to ride his bumper, and honk his horn at him when the traffic was slow. The person rolled their eyes and blew their horn AGAIN and AGAIN! By this time, Joe was frustrated. Honking horns that seemed to be everywhere...warranted and unwarranted, at him and at others.

At the next exit, Joe decided to get off of the interstate and head back home. He pulled in the driveway, parked his car, turned off the ignition, music and GPS, and went into the house. Joe was so sad that he was not going to see his sister, so he began to pray—God gave him a peace that he could not understand. Joe said, *"I can do this because God has given me the strength."* He immediately picked up the phone and made flight arrangements to Jacksonville, Florida. The next day, Joe was on the plane, and in about three hours he was there with his sister waiting for him. And as he expected, there was overwhelming joy and oh how the tears flowed. Joe spent less time traveling and more time bonding with his sister.

Thought for the week: Fear can cause us to miss out on some great experiences, but given the right situation and plenty of prayer, we can muster up the courage. Don't allow fear to keep you from your destination and designed purpose.

What fears have you had to face this week? Are they keeping you from doing something important? Are they keeping you from fulfilling your designed purpose?

_____

_____

_____

_____

_____

_____

_____

_____

_____

_____

_____

_____

_____

Week 28
Handouts or Helping Hands

Handouts or helping hands, which do you give, and is there a difference? Yes, there is a difference—think about it! Giving handouts takes no effort at all. We just hand a person something and move on to the next. We may hand out food, money, biblical tracks, Bibles, etc. to hundreds, but have we taken the time to have a conversation with them whom we've come in contact with? Did we get to know them? Did we find out what they really needed? Giving helping hands takes time and effort. Jesus nor His disciples made it a habit to give handouts. They gave helping hands. They asked questions, found out what the person needed, and extended their hands to help them. ***Their helping hands changed the lives of many and your hands can do the same***.

Thought for the week: People appreciate handouts, but their lives are changed with helping hands. Give a helping hand instead of a handout to someone in need of it.

Did you give a handout or a helping hand this week? Which seemed to help most?

_____

_____

_____

_____

_____

_____

_____

_____

_____

_____

_____

_____

_____

_____

_____

_____

Whose Plan Are You Fulfilling?

We all have plans for our lives, and those plans start very early in life. We are going to be nurses, doctors, teachers, wives, husbands, moms, dads, preachers, and even truck and bus drivers. We are going to graduate from high school and college. We are going to have good jobs and make lots of money, and we are going to travel the world! Our plans sound great and doable, but as we set out to reach our goals something happens—LIFE and REALITY!

The up and downs—hills and valleys—successes and disappointments -- hit us when we least expect it. Some of us struggle in school—it's not as easy as we thought it would be. Some struggle with learning—it's a learning disability. Some experience life's tragedies that leave them in a condition that prohibits them from physically fulfilling their plans. Some experience devastating losses of homes, families, and jobs because of foolish decisions made by them or someone else. Our great plans have been altered, and we have to make new ones to coincide with the lives we have now.

But, just as we have our plans, ***God has plans for us*** too. His plans may not look like the one(s) we have envisioned for ourselves, but they are far better plans—the increasing of His Kingdom. Now don't get it twisted; just like our plans can be altered, God's plan can also be altered. He has given us all deep-seated passions to fulfill His plan; however, as He directs and guides us, we find ourselves using that passion for other purposes. We keep moving further and further away from His plan. We don't think about it, but we are rejecting Him.

If we reject His plan long enough and remain determined to do our own thing in our own way, He will allow that. But believe me, His plan will be done with or without us. This thought is a terrible one, but it's true. If we are not fulfilling the plans of God, dear friends, we are fulfilling the plans of Satan. He has plans for us too!

Thought for the week: God is our creator and He has always had a plan for us. If we look at our lives, we can see Him guiding, preparing, and giving us what we need to fulfill that plan. If you have a deep-seated passion, that's the plan for you! Embrace it and perfect it. He will be there with you all the way to the finish line. Trust Him!

Whose plan have you fulfilled this week? What is your passion? Are you embracing and perfecting it? Can you envision your passion as being one to increase His Kingdom? If not, what is the passion that you feel you can't use to increase His Kingdom? If so, how are you using it to increase His Kingdom?

_____

_____

_____

_____

_____

_____

_____

_____

_____

_____

_____

_____

_____

_____

Week 30
Allow Me to Be Mother

Those title words came to me in one of my quiet moments. I was feeling a sense of disconnect as a mother, so I wrote this poem. I wanted to share it because I'm sure some of the mothers reading this will relate.

Allow me to be mother—to care, to share, and to always be there.

Allow me to be mother—to teach by example that those who learn will give a sample.

Allow me to be mother—to listen with my ears as well as my heart, with hopes that I will forever be a part.

Allow me to be mother—to give proper guidance toward your future, while praying as I follow the Master Tutor.

Allow me to be mother—to work with my hands, but always having the time to put on rubber bands.

Allow me to be mother—to clean, to cook, to wash, and to mend so those in the house on me can depend.

Allow me to be mother—to withstand the test, seeing you grow, mature, and be your best.

Allow me to be mother—to *live and teach the love of God*, the planner of Salvation, and see love grow within you for the ONE who gave Himself for all generations.

SO, ALLOW ME TO BE MOTHER.

Thought for the week: As mothers and fathers, we want the best for our children. We want to see them grow physically, mentally, emotionally, and spiritually. We want them to be successful, responsible adults in this world. While teaching them about their relationship in this world, we MUST be passionately teaching them about their relationship with their Creator (God, His Son, and His spirit). Always remember, *this world is temporary and Heaven and Hell is eternal.*

What have you taught your children (of any age) this week? Are you placing more emphasis on worldly things, on spiritual things, or both? What are you teaching about the world, and what are you teaching about the spirit?

_____

_____

_____

_____

_____

_____

_____

_____

_____

_____

_____

_____

_____

_____

_____

_____

Week 31
Flattering Words: What Good Are They?

Flattering words are powerful when used at the right time and spoken to the right people. We use them more when we want something, want something done, or want something to change. When we want that promotion we think we deserve, we tend to speak flattering words to those who make those decisions. When we want to have a special relationship with that person we've been watching, we speak flattering words that make good impressions. When we want our spouse to do something around the house, we use flattering words to stroke their egos.

Flattery has been used to manipulate, to build false hopes, and to cause a person to carry out misdeeds. So, what good are flattering words, other than the fact that ***people love to hear them*** and they make them feel good?

Thought for the week: People don't need flattering words. They need the TRUTH or nothing at all!

Has someone tried to use flattering words on you this week? If so, what words did they use and why were they used? Did they work and if so, what were the circumstances?

_____

_____

_____

_____

_____

_____

_____

_____

_____

_____

_____

_____

_____

_____

_____

_____

Week 32
God Has Blinders? But He is Spirit!

I'm sure you are now thinking to yourself, how is it that God has blinders when *He is Spirit?* Yes, He is Spirit with spiritual eyes, and along with His spiritual eyes, He has spiritual blinders. Do you ever wonder why He exercises love, patience, peace, kindness, goodness, faithfulness, gentleness, and self-control instead of His wrath when we willfully sin against Him day after day, day after day? Beloved, it's because of His spiritual blinders!

When He gave His son, Jesus Christ, to die for the sins of the world, Christ became His spiritual blinders. When He gave us the Holy Spirit to guide and help us live righteously, the Spirit also became His spiritual blinders. Christ and the Holy Spirit work together as God's spiritual blinders, and when we willfully sin, He does not see us; He sees Christ and the Spirit instead. When *God created man, he became flesh and spirit*. Being flesh and spirit means we have the ability to see physically and spiritually.

So, let me ask: when people sin against us, do we see them through our physical eyes with malice, hatred, impatience, unrighteous judgment, and punishment, or do we put on our spiritual blinders, which help us see and handle them with *kindness, love, patience, righteous judgment, and forgiveness?* Our spiritual blinders cannot be effective unless we are in Christ and being guided by the Spirit.

Thought for the week: We sin against God daily, whether it is through deeds of commission or omission or willfully. Thankfully, He sees us through His spiritual blinders. The Word of God will help expand our spiritual blinders of love, joy, peace, forbearance, kindness, goodness, faithfulness, gentleness, and self-control. When you have them on, try with all your might to keep them on.

Are you walking with your spiritual blinders on this week? If so, which ones? Are you building your spirit with the Word so that you can walk less in the flesh and more in the spirit? What are you doing differently when you walk in the spirit versus walking in the flesh?

_____

_____

_____

_____

_____

_____

_____

_____

_____

_____

_____

_____

_____

_____

_____

_____

_____

Procrastination:
"Friend" or "Foe"

What do you think about procrastination? Most feel that it's a bad trait for one to possess. No one should ever want to be labeled as a procrastinator, and that may be true. But (and yes, I said but), as I thought about that word "procrastination" and looked at the definition (the "act of delaying, or habit of postponing something"), I think that people who think it's a bad trait should consider taking another look. Is it always a "FOE," or can it be a "FRIEND?"

Procrastination—the habit of postponing something—can be a "FOE," especially when something is put off that needs immediate attention. For example: the doctor's visit that could have saved your life through early detection if you had gone long before; the visit/call to a friend who passed away before you contacted them; the study group for a much-needed class, which could have helped you pass, but instead you failed; or that bill you should have paid, and now your home is in jeopardy of foreclosure or lights and water are cut off. There are other things *we put off* or postpone in life that can be detrimental to us physically, mentally, emotionally, and spiritually.

Now, let's look at it from another perspective. Procrastination—the act of delaying—can be a "FRIEND." For example: that wedding proposal and finding out you dodged an emotional bullet; leaving home 15 minutes later than usual and avoiding an accident on the highway; or that certain cruise trip you wanted to take and finding out that same cruise ship had some major issues on the ocean that made everyone ill. There are other things we delay in life that can be helpful to us physically, mentally, emotionally, and spiritually.

Thought for the week: Don't think of procrastination as always bad. It has negative and positive results. You just have to know the difference.

Have you procrastinated this week? Were the results of procrastination positive or negative? If positive results, what were they? If negative results, what were they?

_____

_____

_____

_____

_____

_____

_____

_____

_____

_____

_____

_____

_____

_____

_____

_____

Week 34
The Vision Looking Back at You

When you **look in the mirror**, what vision looks back? Are you seeing clearly, or is your vision distorted? There are beautiful people who look into the mirror and see an unattractive person. There are some who see their reflection as obese and grotesque, but in reality they are thin. Then there are others who see a thin size 8, but in reality they are a size 48. There are other imperfections that seem to give us hard times and also lower the image we have of ourselves. My nose is too big, my hair is too kinky or too thin, my ears are uneven, or my lips are too thin or too thick. I can't stand all of this extra hair on my body. My breasts are too small or too big. I hate my freckles and my moles are hideous. My birthmark is different and it is in a place that draws too much attention. My toes and fingers are short and fat. My hips are too wide and my rear end is enormous. I have a deformity that turns people off. Oh yes I could go on and on but I will stop here. We can't see the **inward beauty** for focusing on the outward appearance.

Who is to blame for the negative way we see ourselves? I blame Society, which tries to set the standards for everything! It even has a standard for how we should look. If we slow down and take conscious notice, we can see it everywhere. It's displayed on TV, in newspaper ads, magazines, and department stores; we see it while walking down the streets. What's sad is that Society is not only infiltrating the minds of adults, it's infecting the minds of our children from an early age. Even our children can do and say some very hurtful things to each other when Society's standards are not followed. There have been times that people have taken very extreme measures to change what they see as imperfections.

If you are one who looks into the mirror and sees a distorted image, quickly look away and **_remember who you are and who created you_**. The God of Heaven created you in His image, and His image is definitely not distorted. He does not see the outward appearance of man/woman; He sees the inward image. When you realize your inward beauty, the next time you look in the mirror you will clearly see the person you really are—a beautiful creation of God.

Thought for the week: God creates no imperfections outwardly or inwardly. Society has created the image for us, and we have fallen right into the trap of trying to fit into that image. Remember, God is the image standard setter—He makes everyone in His image. Teach this to your children, they will need it and will appreciate you for showing and helping them to see the real them.

What image did you see looking back at you from the mirror this week? Was it a clear image or a distorted one? Why was it clear or distorted? Whose standards did you use—the standards of God or the standards that society sets?

_____

_____

_____

_____

_____

_____

_____

_____

_____

_____

_____

_____

_____

_____

_____

_____

Week 35
Early Morn

I wrote this poem when enjoying a quiet moment one early morn. I was sitting on my couch looking out of the window. This is what came to my mind.

Look out and enjoy the early morn. See the stillness, the quiet that it brings.

Look up and see the sky that God so carefully painted with infinite wisdom and passionate desire.

See God's loving care as you watch the birds eat what and all they want, get their fill, and take flight without a care.

God has made the early morn for His creations. Enjoy; take advantage of it. You may find yourself engulfed with the ***confidence of God's love***, and the calmness and tranquility of the day.

Thought for the week: God has created everything for man to survive and to enjoy. Take a few minutes out of your day and witness the beauty of the sky, and watch creation do what it was created to do. It is an amazing sight.

Did you look up at the sky or watch creation this week?
What are you witnessing? How does it make you feel?

True Friends: Who Has Them?

Do you have a true *friend?* If so, you are a blessed and rich person. Not everybody has true friends. They are poor in this area because: (1) they don't know how to choose them; (2) they don't know the difference between true friends and acquaintances; and (3) they don't know how to be true friends themselves. Young people call everyone they come in contact with their friends, but they are actually acquaintances. True friends are special and hard to find because the qualities that they possess are so rare.

Not everyone has what it takes to be a true friend—it can be very challenging. It requires unconditional love, compassion, giving, and patience, as well as backbone and stamina. True friends love you when you are not showing love. They are there when no one else is. They are dependable; they can always be counted on. They tell you the truth even though it may hurt. A true friend always wants the best for you. ***They stick closer to you than a brother or sister.*** They are there in times of sadness and happiness. They cry with you in your failures and celebrate with you in your successes. They are always encouraging and sparking that fire within you. They know just the right things to say at just the right time.

Now, here is the challenge; you must also be a true friend.

Thought for the week: Not everyone is your true friend, and it is our responsibility to teach our young people the same. Don't use "true friend" loosely. When you have one, you have a rare jewel—cherish it.

Evaluate the qualities of your friend(s) this week. Are they your "true friends" or acquaintances? Whose "true friend" are you? Are you treating your true friends like the precious gems they are?

_____

_____

_____

_____

_____

_____

_____

_____

_____

_____

_____

_____

_____

_____

_____

Week 37
Weight of Life

I understand that the weight of life is trying to cause your spirit to sink, but praise be to God you have not drowned.

God's Spirit is holding you afloat no matter how heavy the weight of life may be. The weight is trying very hard to pull and hold you down.

I pray that you will hold fast and **when you have endured,** you can look back and see that God was working with you to do greater works that are ahead.

God will always be with you as you float over and ride the turbulence that is causing this weight of life.

Thought for the week: Life is full of trouble and tribulation. Sometimes they get so heavy that we begin to lose heart. Be of good cheer, my dear friend, because God will not let you go through anything that you cannot bear.

What is your weight of life this week? What are you doing to bear it? What are you doing to lighten it?

_____

_____

_____

_____

_____

_____

_____

_____

_____

_____

_____

_____

_____

_____

_____

_____

_____

_____

Exodus From Bondage

I compare our Exodus from the bondage of sin to the Hebrews' Exodus from the bondage of the Egyptians. The Hebrews were being tormented daily by their oppressors and we as God's children are tormented by the oppressors of trials, tribulations, and sin. God told the Hebrews what to do to prepare for the Exodus and He tells us what to do to prepare for our Exodus. The Hebrews followed every command given and their escape from bondage was a success. Even though they escaped the bondage, that did not mean that they were not going to be ***faced with trials and tribulations, and would not have to fight some battles on their way to claim what God had promised them***. They even had dire consequences to face because of their sin of disobedience—God had to do some purging. After the purging, the Hebrews received the land that flowed with milk and honey. Oh, what a glorious day!

We will have our trials and tribulations to face, and we will have to fight some battles. We will have consequences to face because of our sins—which means we or God will have to do some purging. But, if we follow God's commands, we can be successful in our Exodus. He has made us a promise as well. He has a place for us that also flows with milk and honey—that place is Heaven. The day will come when we can claim it, and oh what a glorious day that will be!

Thought for the week: We are becoming stronger and stronger as we face each trial and tribulation. We are being prepared for our Exodus from the bondage of sins so that we can one day claim our land flowing with milk and honey. Don't give up—stay strong, pray, and continue to trust and obey.

What bondage are you preparing an Exodus from this week? Has it been hard to prepare for your Exodus? If so, why? What will you do differently to begin your preparation?

_____

_____

_____

_____

_____

_____

_____

_____

_____

_____

_____

_____

_____

_____

_____

_____

_____

Describing God

How do we describe God? There are so many words that we use to describe Him, and many of them are found right in His Word: *love, truth, faithful, all powerful, a consuming fire, is jealous, merciful, great, awesome, God of gods and Lord or lords, our refuge, eternal*, and the list goes on. These are words that describe His character, words we can understand with our finite minds. However, they do not accurately describe Him. Some have gone as far as creating new words, such as an expert, accurate, excelling, unequaled, spotless, effectual, realistic, and valid; and again the list goes on. It amuses me because we try to describe God with words, but no matter how many words we come up with, none will ever totally describe Him. God is spirit and He is beyond description—He just IS!

Thought for the week: God is a spirit and we can only describe His character. There is no need to try to describe Him because it will be futile.

IN YOUR QUIET MOMENTS

Did you try describing God this week? What words did you use? Did you use those that are written in the Word, or did you come up your own? If so, what were they?

_____

_____

_____

_____

_____

_____

_____

_____

_____

_____

_____

_____

_____

_____

Out of Sight Out of Mind

I have heard this saying from a child, and as the words penetrate my mind and I think about the changes in life, I can understand how it can be true. If I may say, and I believe this—a parent whose children left home to build lives themselves must have come up with this saying. At first, they made calls to each other every day, then it became once a week, then on holidays, then on birthdays. After some years, the yearly vacations with the parents became family vacations, their families. Then holidays and traditions with parents became family holidays and traditions, with their families. The phone calls as well as the visits became less and less frequent. Why does this happen?

The more life gives us, the busier we become. The more distractions and trials we face, the less we want to think about and deal with. Most times, we pay closer attention to what is in front of us and less attention to those things that are not.

So, what's happening to the connection of those whose bond should never be broken? What's happening when life goes on and parents and children are no longer in each other's lives? What's happening when grandparents don't know their grandchildren and the grandchildren don't know them? Why is the family connection broken? I will say, "OUT OF SIGHT OUT OF MIND!" If this is happening in your family, be determined not to allow it. It is imperative that you try very hard to make some changes that will keep your family connected. Family is all we have. And you know what? The same thing tends to happen to the relationship between God and His children; "OUT OF SIGHT OUT OF MIND," and we know why.

Thought for the week: When we don't stay connected to our family members on a regular basis, we tend not to think about them as much. The same thing happens to our relationship with God. The less time we spend with Him, the less connected we become. No connection, no relationship. Keep connected with family and with God.

IN YOUR QUIET MOMENTS

Were you connected to your family and to God this week? Who did you connect with that you hadn't thought about in a while? How long has it been since the last time you connected with family and with God?

Hey! Who Are You Listening To?

We listen to so many people. We listen to our parents, our family members, our peers, our friends, our preachers, and most of the time we listen to ourselves. Are we listening to what tickles our ears? Are we really listening to what's being said to us? Are we being told the truth? People tend to tell us their truth. They are fallible—they are capable of lying to us, and more often than not, we even lie to ourselves. God is infallible—He will tell us the truth and nothing but the truth because *He can't lie.* So, since He can't lie, we need not listen to people who do, but instead to Him who can't. So find His truth where it's found—in His Word.

Thought for the week: No one wants to be lied to. Listen very closely to what you are being told; sometimes those things can be questionable. If you don't want to be lied to, then don't lie to others. Deciphering the truth can sometimes be difficult. In times like this, seek God for help.

Who are you listening to this week? Did they tell you the truth, and did you know that it was the truth? Were people listening to you and did you tell them the truth?

_____

_____

_____

_____

_____

_____

_____

_____

_____

_____

_____

_____

_____

_____

_____

Week 42
Wisdom Is Applied Knowledge

I have heard this statement before, that "Wisdom is applied knowledge"; for some reason, when I heard it one day, it touched my spirit. Wisdom is something I want to have, and I'm sure you do too. Wisdom is when you APPLY the knowledge you have acquired to your life. However, wisdom will not come to us in totality because we are always acquiring more and more knowledge (learning new things) everyday.

I hate to admit it, but I don't always apply what I learn to my life. It may be something that is hard because it requires changing, or maybe I've decided that I just don't want to do it. The Word says that **wisdom comes from God**. God supplies knowledge and then He gives you the strength to apply it to your life. I have to remember that **knowing and not applying is not wisdom...it's foolishness!**

Thought for the week: Acquiring knowledge is simple because we are always learning new things, but applying what we learn can be difficult. When the difficult times come and you are not applying the things you learn, ask God for help.

IN YOUR QUIET MOMENTS

What did you learn this week? Are you applying what you are learning to your life? If you did not apply the knowledge, what's hindering you?

_____

_____

_____

_____

_____

_____

_____

_____

_____

_____

_____

_____

_____

_____

_____

_____

_____

Week 43

Lord, It's Just Too Much!

Doing, doing, doing—going, going, going. And it's all for everyone else—husband, wife, children, grandchildren, parents, grandparents, extended family, supervisor, coworkers. This is my life, but Lord, it's too much! When can I get a break? Do people realize I get tired? Being pulled in many directions, by too many people—I'm being drained. And on top of all this, some of my family members and friends are sick and dying! And my health is beginning to decline. Lord, it's too much—the heartbreak—the stress. Lord, it's just too much!

Through all the tears and stress, I'm reminded of what can help me get through these times—taking some real time with YOU. I feel a sense of relief when I remember how refreshed I am when I take this time. I remember your promise that *you don't give us any more than we can bear or handle.* This I believe! I'm so thankful for times to reflect on YOU so that I can regroup and catch my breath.

Thought for the week: God knows all we face on a daily basis. He knows how much we can bear, and He gives us what we need to get through. Reflect on His Word and pray without ceasing. It helps!

Who and what things have come up this week that is causing you stress and heartache? Who and what things have come up that have altered your plans/schedule? How did you handle them?

_____

_____

_____

_____

_____

_____

_____

_____

_____

_____

_____

_____

_____

_____

Week 44
Godly Mentorship

If you have or have had a godly mother, grandmother, or mentor in your life, you have truly been blessed. In my quiet moment, I remember that I have been blessed over the years to have godly examples, but I have to confess that I didn't always appreciate them or their guidance. I let them know by not listening, being rebellious, and acting rude. During these times of rebellion and rudeness, I saw so much disappointment and hurt in their eyes, but even that didn't move me to do what was right. I missed so many lessons and made plenty of mistakes. But, praise God, *I allowed Him to open my eyes* to how important it was for me growing up to have godly people in my life, and more so that I changed my life and became one of them.

You may be saying to yourself, "I don't/didn't have a godly mother, grandmother, or mentor in my life." I say to you, don't be discouraged, but seek God and his righteousness, and learn to become one for someone else. Be a blessing from God—many will benefit and learn valuable lessons from you. If you happen to get someone like me, don't give up. Pray for them, and they will one day come to their senses.

Thought for the week: Being a godly mentor is not easy, but the blessings are great. You may get rejected, but keep mentoring, encouraging, and praying. You may not be appreciated right now, but you will be in time. You will be blessed as you witness them becoming godly mentors as well.

Are you giving godly mentoring this week? If so, who is it, and what godly mentoring did you give? Are you being rejected and unappreciated? In what ways are these being performed in action?

_____

_____

_____

_____

_____

_____

_____

_____

_____

_____

_____

_____

_____

_____

To Yourself Be Honest

I know there have been times you have asked yourself, to whom can I really be honest? I can't be honest with family and friends because it will hurt them. I can't be honest with spiritual family because ***it may bring JUDGMENT!*** I can't be honest with myself because sometimes it brings pain, sorrow and hurtful memories. And when I'm honest with God, I feel guilt and shame. I don't want to feel any painful emotion. I don't want to be judged! And most of all, I don't want to feel guilt and shame. So, what do I do? I hold close the truths that I don't want others to know, and I bury other truths to keep from myself.

What makes us feel the need to hold close some truths and bury others? We tend to hold close those things that could hurt someone, or ruin the reputation and image we have tried so long to uphold. We bury others because they bring us deep, personal pain. This pain can be overwhelming, so we hide these truths by burying them deep within ourselves, hoping they won't surface. However, over time, someway and somehow the truth will re-enter our minds like a crashing wave at high-tide that can make us feel as though we are drowning. Some truths can be so devastating that the memory of them frighten us, make us cry, and even make some of us mentally ill.

All truths will come out! So, dear friends, you have to prepare yourself for these revealing truths by first being honest with the two who know you best God and You. When facing truth, there are a couple of things to remember: (1) don't judge yourself when you are honest with yourself; and (2) don't allow guilt and shame to keep you from being honest with God. When you are honest with God and yourself, you will be more inclined to be honest with others.

Thought for the week: To yourself and God be true. Bury your truth and be a prisoner; confess it, and be free. The truth WILL set you free. All prisoners desire freedom!

Have you tried being honest with yourself and God this week? What things are you truthful about? Are there any emotions, pain, or consequences you're facing because of the truth? How do you feel after you share your truth and acknowledge it?

_____

_____

_____

_____

_____

_____

_____

_____

_____

_____

_____

_____

_____

_____

_____

_____

Don't Be So Quick to Judge

In my quiet moment, I remember a day, several years ago, when I went into the store. As I stepped up to the cashier, I realized by the expression on her face and by her body language that she was not going to be pleasant. I was not feeling my best either that day, and Satan knew it. He is always looking for ways to tempt God's creation and, this was a perfect situation that he could use at the time.

She was very rude and had an attitude when I spoke to her. I asked if she was having a bad day, but this lady did not respond. Her behavior affected me to the point that I wanted to put my groceries back in the cart and go to another checkout line, but I had too many items to put back. I could actually feel my blood pressure going up. I thought to myself, "Lady, you are in the wrong position. You need a job where you don't have to be around people." She proceeded to check me out and said nothing—she hardly looked at me. ***Instead of reporting her to the manager, I left the store angry.*** I knew I needed to pray, and I did pray for her and myself that day.

The next day, I purposefully went back to the store; to my relief, she was there. So, with no groceries to check out, I went through her line. I had a card in hand, gave it to her with a smile, and walked away. The next time I saw her, she gave me a big hug and said thank you. What a beautiful lesson this taught me and I hope her as well. Days are not always good ones, and they are not promised to be. But when they aren't, still continue to ***love and treat others like you want to be*** *treated,* and, most of all, ***don't be so quick to judge because you will be judged too!***

Thought for the week: When you are faced with challenging days, remember that these days are a good time for Satan to play his hand. Don't play the hand he deals you.

IN YOUR QUIET MOMENTS

What challenges are you facing this week? How are you handling them? Do you see God or Satan at work? What lessons are you learning?

_____

_____

_____

_____

_____

_____

_____

_____

_____

_____

_____

_____

_____

_____

_____

_____

_____

I Want True Love—What About You?

I have heard it said that love comes to those who wait, and I believe it. I've learned that when we wait, we open ourselves to God's guidance and to the one He has intended for us. When we wait, God gives us the ability to see things that are important for a lasting relationship. He shows us through example what true love is, what it looks like, and how we are to love truly.

However, when we rush, we don't allow God to guide our lives. We go our own way, looking for love in the wrong places, and life-altering mistakes are sometimes made. We also miss the important signs and the way of escape that God provides—signs that say out loud, "RUN!" But because we want love so badly, we hear the loud warnings of "Run," but Satan drowns it out with a louder "DON'T RUN."

Don't look for love in the wrong places; listen to and take heed of the warning signs, and allow the only expert on LOVE to guide you.

Thought for the week: God is love and this love is identified and expressed in His Word. Give this LOVE and others will be blessed; receive this LOVE and you will be blessed. Everyone wants True Love.

Who are you loving this week? How are you exemplifying this love? Are you being loved? How is it being shown to you? Are you paying attention to the warning signs, or are you ignoring them? Are you the one that someone needs to be warned about?

_____

_____

_____

_____

_____

_____

_____

_____

_____

_____

_____

_____

_____

_____

_____

_____

The Exit Signs of Life

Do you approach the exit signs of life as you approach the ones on the highway? Do you drive slowly and watch for the signs, and as you approach them, take your time and slowly get off the ramp? Or do you allow speed and distractions such as cell phones, loud music, conversing with passengers, and the like to cause you to miss the signs and speed right by those exit ramps? If so, you'll **find yourself getting off on the wrong ramp. This ramp is taking you in a direction and to a place you don't want to end up.** As you travel, there are multiple opportunities for you to turn around, but you keep going in the wrong direction. The longer you travel that way, the further away you are from your intended destination. You'll find yourself never getting there.

The way we approach the exit signs on the highway is the same way we approach the exit signs of life. We approach them slowly, or we approach quickly and miss them entirely because of distractions (sin). While we are traveling, some of the exit signs are very clear, and we approach them slowly and with caution. We want to make sure we get off at the right exit ramp so we can arrive at our destination. Sometimes the distractions in our life make the exit signs unclear, and we speed right passed them. There are multiple opportunities to turn around, but those same distractions keep our vision blurred. One day we will look up to find that we have been going the wrong way for years—never turning around, never getting off, and never making it to our destination HEAVEN.

Thought for the week: God is directing us to Heaven, and His directions are very clear and precise. Follow them, and if you get off the wrong exit, don't delay; turn around immediately.

Have you had to turn around because you were going in the wrong direction? Where were you going? How long did it take you to realize you were going the wrong way? Which GPS is directing you?

_____

_____

_____

_____

_____

_____

_____

_____

_____

_____

_____

_____

_____

_____

_____

_____

Week 49
The GPS's

When we travel, we want to make sure that we get to our destination. Whether it's traveling short distances in the local area or long distances across the country, we want to make sure that we get there without any stress of getting lost. There is a system on most cell phones and in some cars called the Global Positioning System (GPS) that will get you where you want to go. It can tell you from starting point to destination how long it will take, the condition of the roads, the weather conditions, and the shortest way to get there. It even gives the different routes you can take—highway or scenic. And if you get off course, it will immediately tell you to turn around, or it will recalculate your directions. I would say it is a pretty smart device, but it has a flaw; it is manmade. It can break down, stop working, or malfunction. When it does, you will have to go back to old faithful; the old paper map. I will also say that we put too much confidence and trust in this manmade device.

Now, there is a GPS that you may want to investigate and consider. It can be trusted and all confidence can be put in it. It will never fail you, never break down, and never malfunction. However, there is something you may want to know: this GPS has only one destination in its system, so if you have another destination in mind, don't even think about plugging that address in because, it will not compute. If you intentionally get off course, or if you get lost, this GPS will infallibly redirect you. ***The destination is Heaven and you can only get there by using this GPS (God's Positioning System): THE BIBLE.***

Thought for the week: Remember, there is only one destination that God's Positioning System (GPS) can direct you toward. If your destination is somewhere other than Heaven (and we know there is only one other place), the GPS can definitely tell you to change your course. When you do, it will direct to you Heaven.

Have you been off course or lost this week? Where were you going? Did you have to use the GPS? Which one did you use?

_____

_____

_____

_____

_____

_____

_____

_____

_____

_____

_____

_____

_____

_____

_____

_____

_____

Week 50
Words of Wisdom:
Do You Know Them?

Has anyone ever come to you with a negative opinion about someone you have never met or haven't had the chance to get to know? Well, if it hasn't happened, it will. While you were being told their opinion, did you add your comments to the conversation of what you heard about the person from someone else? ***How do you think they would feel if they knew you were speaking negatively about them?*** Better yet, how you would feel if the shoe was on the other foot and the conversation was about you? Let me encourage you not to listen to negative opinions about someone; from these words, you will most likely form the same negative opinion before you meet that person or get to know them.

The day now comes and you get the chance to meet that person. Instead of a fresh, first-time meeting experience, you've got this cloud in your mind, and you can't see them for the person they really are—and you really don't want to take the time to get to know them. Why? Because "you already know how they are." When someone comes to you with a negative opinion about someone, say, "Please keep that to yourself, I would like to be able to form my own opinion." Thank them and change the subject.

Thought for the week: If a person comes to you with negative, unsolicited opinions about someone, believe me—they are bringing negative opinions about you to someone else. Don't form your opinion on the negatives perceived by someone else. You may miss out on a long, lasting, and rewarding friendship.

Has anyone come to you this week with negative opinion about someone? Did you go to them with negative opinion about someone else? If you listened to the negative opinions, whose friendship did you miss out on? If you didn't listen, how have you been blessed by your new friendship?

_____

_____

_____

_____

_____

_____

_____

_____

_____

_____

_____

_____

_____

_____

_____

_____

Week 51
Admirers or Tormentors

When someone is in the public's eye, there are two types of people who give them what they need to grow: the Admirers and the Tormentors. They can both promote and hinder your growth physically, mentally, emotionally, and spiritually. It's up to you which one it will be; promote or hinder. It's a blessing for someone to admire your accomplishments and give you accolades, but it can hinder your growth when you allow the admiration to make you arrogant and conceited. You are now walking in the clouds and looking down on everyone else. ***You start thinking more of yourself than of others.*** However, it can promote your growth when you become thankful and humble for what God has allowed you, and for what you can do for others.

Then there are the tormentors who can make it more difficult to promote growth. They spew out jealous remarks to hurt, belittle, and downplay what God has allowed you to accomplish. They have no encouragement to give—only discouragement—and this can hinder your growth when you allow it to depress and stagnate you. You stop doing the task(s) God has given you, and nothing more is accomplished.

Tormentors are given too much power. On the other hand, they can promote your growth as you feed on what they do. Their actions can inspire and make you more determined to continue to the task(s). You ask God to help you more so that you can do even more for others.

Thought for the week: Admirers can promote or hinder your growth. Tormentors can also promote or hinder your growth. Promote or Hinder—it's up to you to decide which.

Did you have any admirers or tormentors in your life this week? Did you allow admirers and tormentors to promote or hinder your growth? What task(s) did you stop when you allowed them to hinder your growth? What task(s) were carried on when you allowed them to promote your growth? Now, here's a hard question: Were you the admirer or the tormentor?

_____

_____

_____

_____

_____

_____

_____

_____

_____

_____

_____

_____

_____

_____

Week 52

Who's There for Them?

Too many times have I seen the sadness, weariness, and downcast countenance in the eyes and faces of elders, deacons, preachers, teachers, and some members of the Body of Christ who needed someone to talk to. They have been there for so many, but when it's their turn, who's there for them? They need someone to help them bear their burdens. They need encouragement. They need a shoulder to cry on. They need comforting. But who is there? No one!

You may say that they have family members, and I say to you, so do the people that they are there for. You also may also ask, of all the people they come in contact with, why isn't anyone there for them? And I ask you, why aren't you?

Yes, they listen and shoulder the burdens of so many. That's what they do because they are leaders. They listen and shoulder. They have no one because they are the rocks for so many. People don't realize that these leaders have problems too. They don't share because they will be looked upon as a weak leader and having no business being in the position they are in. They will be judged. They have to be very cautious and careful what they share and with whom; if they have to be that cautious and careful, they don't share with anyone. Why do they have to carry their own burdens too? Yes, they have God, and so do the people that come to them. Just as others need someone so do they—so, I ask, why can't it be you? Ask yourself, why can't it be me?

Thought for the week: So many leaders are deprived of someone to help shoulder their burdens and talk to. Why can't it be you? Prepare yourself to be there for anyone who comes to you for a listening ear.

Did you need a trustworthy ear this week? Who did you choose to be the listener? Were they open to your concerns, or did you feel as though you were being judged? Did someone choose you as a listener? Did you judge them?

_____

_____

_____

_____

_____

_____

_____

_____

_____

_____

_____

_____

_____

_____

_____

_____

A Prayer of Gratitude

Dear gracious Father, the Creator of the heavens and the earth, and everything in it. I come before your throne this day, this hour, this moment in a spirit of humbleness thanking you for every blessing you have given us. I thank you for the loving sacrifice of your dear Son Jesus Christ. Love moved You to send Him to this cruel earth to live and to experience, in the flesh, the things that your most precious creation (mankind) experience. Love moved Your Son to willingly offer His body to suffer, to bleed, and to die on the cross—not for His sins, but for our sins. Thank you, Father, for raising Him from the dead which gives us hope that if we live faithful to You, we will have the opportunity to live with You throughout eternity. Father, I thank you.

I want to thank You for guiding me and giving me the thoughts that are written in this Devotional Journal. Thank You for the people You placed in my life who encouraged me throughout this journey.

I thank You for each person who is taking the time out of their busy schedule to read and to journal. I pray each week's thought will inspire, encourage, and motivate them to journal their own thoughts, and to reference Holy Bible scriptures for all biblical principles. And most of all, I pray that we will all move closer to You, to your Son, and be open to the guidance of Your Spirit.

Father, continue to bless us all with food, clothing, and shelter. Bless us with good health, sound minds, and gentle spirits. In Jesus' Name I pray, Amen.

Father, thank you for hearing the prayer of your child,
Alwanda

74682986R00107

Made in the USA
Columbia, SC
04 August 2017